AUGUSTA READ THOMAS

T0087626

SHAKIN'

HOMAGE TO ELVIS PRESLEY AND IGOR STRAVINSKY

ED 4297
First Printing: September 2006

ISBN-13: 978-1-4234-1644-9

ISBN-10: 1-4234-1644-9

G. SCHIRMER, Inc.

DISTRIBUTED BY

HAL•LEONARD®
CORPORATION
7777 W. BLUEMOUND RD. P.O. BOX 13819 MILWAUKEE, WI 53213

*Shakin' was commissioned by
the Memphis Symphony Orchestra, David Loebel, Music Director,
and the Music Library Association in honor of its 75th Anniversary.*

*The first performance was given by the Memphis Symphony Orchestra
under the direction of David Loebel on 24 February 2006.*

Performance Notes:

Grace notes come before the beat.

Strings to be plucked inside the piano are indicated as *pizz.*
this is cancelled with *ord.* The piano should be located with
the percussion in the back of the orchestra.

Divisi sections in the strings should always be split as inside
and outside.

Eight violins require practice mutes.

String bowing suggestions and preferences are marked by
the composer but can be altered at the discretion of the
players and conductor.

Music of many periods and by different composers and improvisers has fascinated and nurtured me since I was a child. I deeply love the music of J.S. Bach for its precision, its amazing invention, its elegance, and the nobility and grandeur of its emotional spectrum. Bach sounds utterly modern to me, even 300 years after it was composed. The music of a myriad of other composers and Blues, Rock, and Jazz improvisers keeps me focused and humble at the same time as they inspire me with confidence for creative thinking.

Shakin' pays homage to Elvis and Stravinsky. I grew up in the 1960s, the 10th of 10 children (and a twin), in a home with music playing in literally every room! All my brothers and sisters loved Rock and Roll and so did I, and thus, at a very deep level, it has indisputably affected my music.

Shakin' is a six-minute work for orchestra, which falls into two short sections, played without a pause. The first is characterized by the use of soloists in the orchestra. It is lyric and elegant, and tuneful. Eight solo violinists, all who have practice mutes on their instruments (which makes their sound extremely dreamy, distant, and delicate) play brief song fragments. They spin an eight-part counterpoint-web. This dreamy lattice obscures each song, so one should not try to hear "Amazing Grace," for instance, but it is in there, floating above the orchestra in the soloists, as if to recall the web of power that Elvis holds on us all, from afar.

The second half of the work is one long crescendo, from *ppp* to *ffff*, and it also is a gradual and continual accelerando. There are several "licks" that repeat, although subjected to slight variations, and give a feeling of a transformed Rock and Roll motive.

—Augusta Read Thomas

Instrumentation

Piccolo
2 Flutes
2 Oboes
English Horn
3 Clarinets in B flat (3rd doubling Bass Clarinet)
Alto Saxophone in E flat
2 Bassoons (2nd doubling Contrabassoon)

4 Horns in F
3 Trumpets in C (optional Trumpet 1 doubling on Piccolo Trumpet in B flat)
Trombone
Bass Trombone
Tuba

Percussion (3 players)
    (Unless otherwise specified, please use the most common mallet or beater)

    I. vibraphone (motor on at times, 1 bow needed), very large triangle, medium suspended cymbal, 2 bongos, 2 low conga drums

    II. crotales (2 octaves, 1 bow needed), tubular chimes (shared with Percussion 3), large triangle, large suspended cymbal, very large bass drum

    III. glockenspiel, tubular chimes (shared with Percussion 2), small triangle, small suspended cymbal (bow needed), sizzle cymbal, chinese cymbal, 3 low tom-toms (graduated in pitch: very low, low, and moderately low)

Piano
Harp

Strings (approx. 14,11,9,8,7)

duration ca. 6 minutes

Performance material is available on rental from the publisher.
G. Schirmer/AMP Rental and Performance Department
P.O. Box 572
Chester, NY 10918
(845) 469-4699 - phone
(845) 469-7544 - fax
www.schirmer.com

Information on Augusta Read Thomas and her works is available at www.schirmer.com

with admiration and gratitude to the Music Library Association, David Loebel, and The Memphis Symphony Orchestra

SHAKIN'

Homage to Elvis Presley and Igor Stravinsky

Augusta Read Thomas
(2006)

Note: The 8 violin soloists, with practice mutes on, should sound like a distant, floating web of lyric lines. They fade in and out of prominence, depending on the loudness and texture of the orchestra. They should *not* sound like foreground solos.

*From measure 18, only the Violoncelli and Contrabassi are *not* muted.

Perpetual (with repetition and variations) motion

* From here to the end, there is a very gradual *accellerando* from ♩ = 96 to ♩ = 144.
In addition, from here to the end is one long crescendo.

9